Make Understanding

The Big Red Heart

Super Easy!

Z.B. Tucker

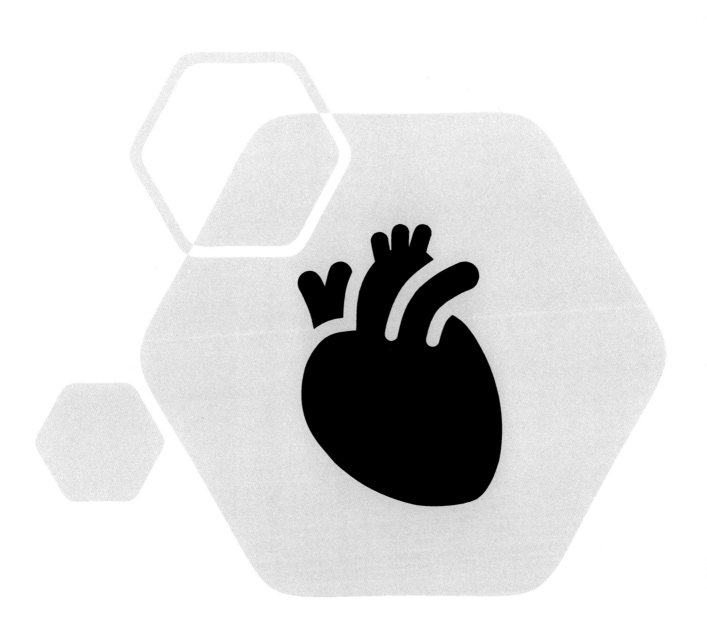

Table of Content

What is the Human Heart?

The human heart is a large muscle. The heart works like a pump, for it pumps and moves blood throughout the body.

Your heart

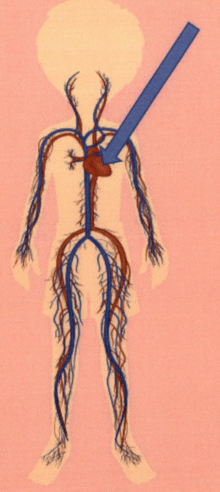

Why is the heart so important to the human body?

The heart is important because it pumps oxygen and blood throughout your body. It is the central command center for your body's blood system. Without oxygen and blood, the body cannot survive. Your blood is important because it carries oxygen through your body.

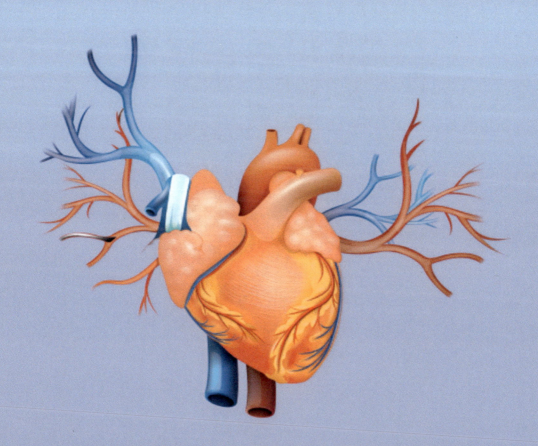

How big is the heart?

The average human heart is about the size of a closed fist. Sometimes the heart can grow bigger depending on a person's size, health, and age. The average heart weighs about seven to fifteen ounces.

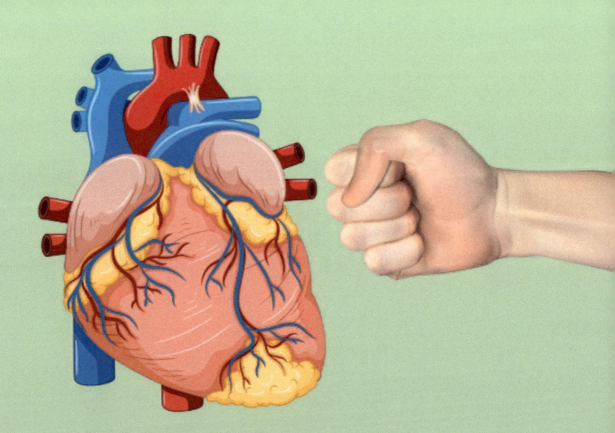

What is the shape of the heart?

The heart is shaped like an upside-down pear or like a pinecone.

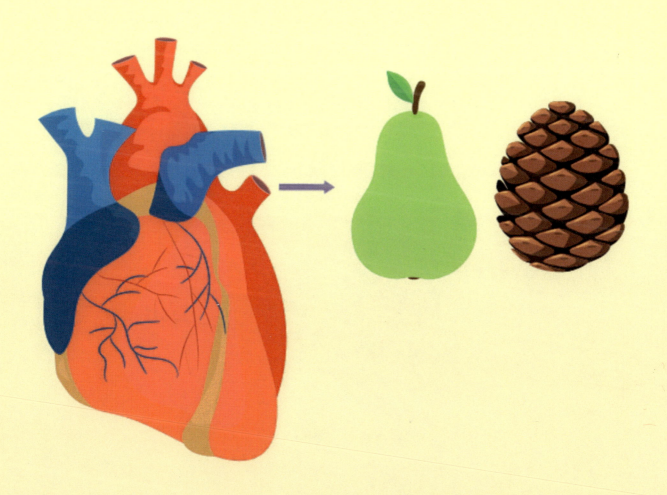

Where is the heart located?

The heart is located in the center of the chest and lays between the two lungs. It is protected by a bone called the sternum which sits in front of the heart to provide protection from injury.

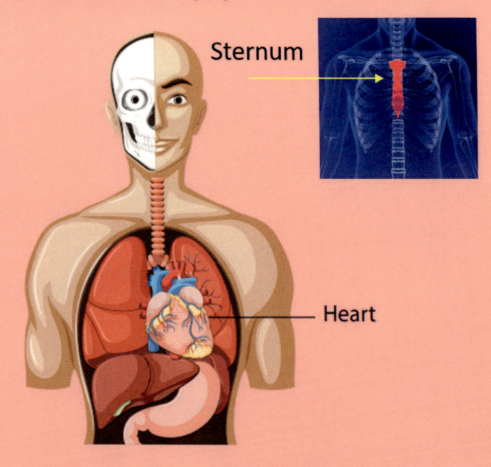

Sternum

Heart

What are the parts of the heart?

The heart is divided into a left side and a right side. This is to keep blood that has oxygen separated from the blood which does not have oxygen.

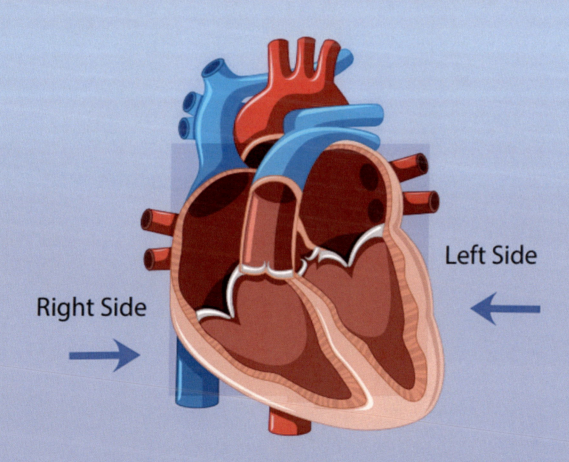

Right Side

Left Side

What is the difference between the left heart and the right heart?

The left side of the heart receives blood that has oxygen in it. The right side of the heart receives blood that does not have oxygen. Each side of the heart is made up of chambers.

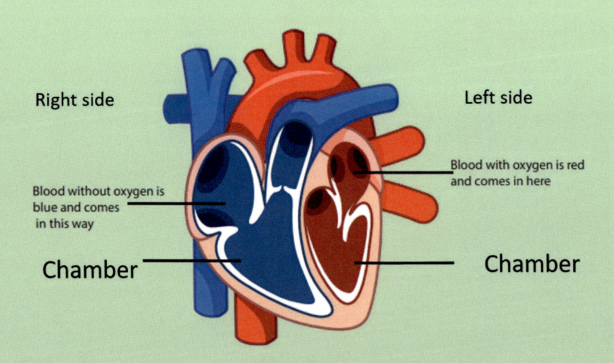

Right side

Left side

Blood with oxygen is red and comes in here

Blood without oxygen is blue and comes in this way

Chamber

Chamber

What are the heart chambers?

Think of the heart chambers like a four-bedroom house with two rooms on the first floor and two rooms on the second floor. The heart is made up of these four chambers, two at the top and two at the bottom. The two upper chambers of the heart are called atria. The two lower chambers of the heart are called the ventricles.

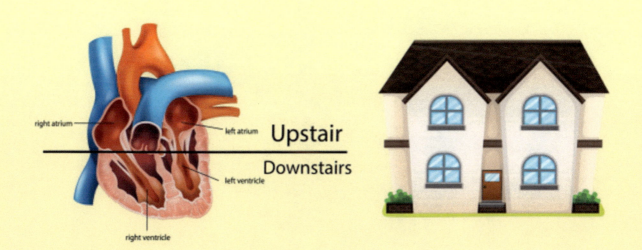

right atrium

left atrium   Upstair

Downstairs

left ventricle

right ventricle

What do the heart chambers do?

Each heart chamber acts as a holding station and is responsible for keeping a certain amount of blood until the heart is ready to pump the blood back throughout the body at the right time.
Blood enters the heart through the upper chambers and exits the heart through the lower chambers.

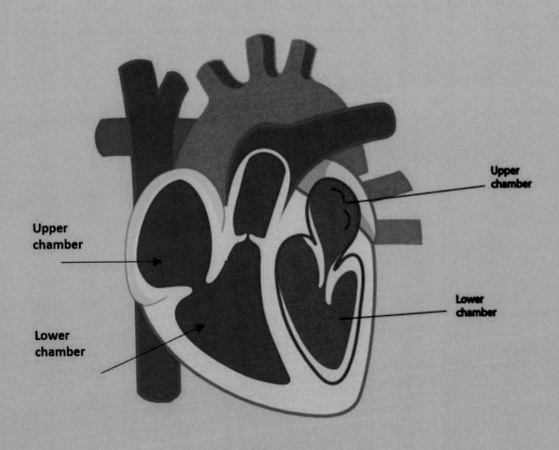

Upper chamber

Lower chamber

Upper chamber

Lower chamber

How does the heart pump blood?

The heart receives an electrical signal that allows it to begin a heartbeat. A heartbeat is when the heart expands and contracts or relaxes back to its normal position again. These two movements, expand and contract, create the two heart beats, thump, thump.

View Inside your heart:

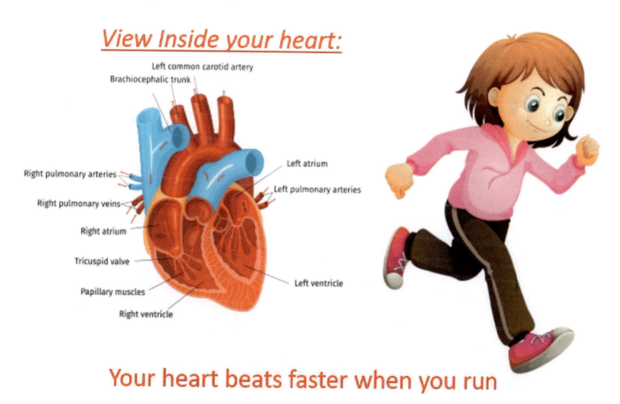

Left common carotid artery

Brachiocephalic trunk

Right pulmonary arteries

Right pulmonary veins

Right atrium

Tricuspid valve

Papillary muscles

Right ventricle

Left atrium

Left pulmonary arteries

Left ventricle

Your heart beats faster when you run

What happens when the heart expands and contracts?

When the heart expands it allows blood to enter the atria heart chambers and when the heart relaxes, it allows blood to leave the ventricles to go into different parts of the body. Each time the heart beats, it is moving or circulating blood in and out of the heart and throughout the entire body.

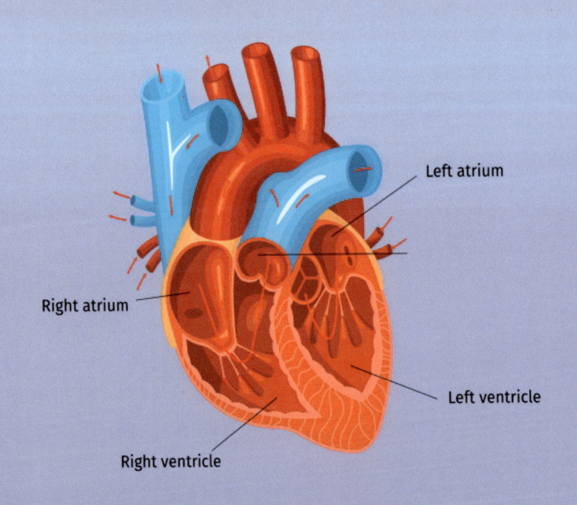

Left atrium

Right atrium

Left ventricle

Right ventricle

How does blood flow into the heart?

Blood comes into the heart from the right side of the body through the right atria, then into the right ventricle of the heart. The blood that enters the right side of the heart does not have oxygen yet, so the heart pumps this blood out of the right ventricle and into the lungs to receive oxygen.

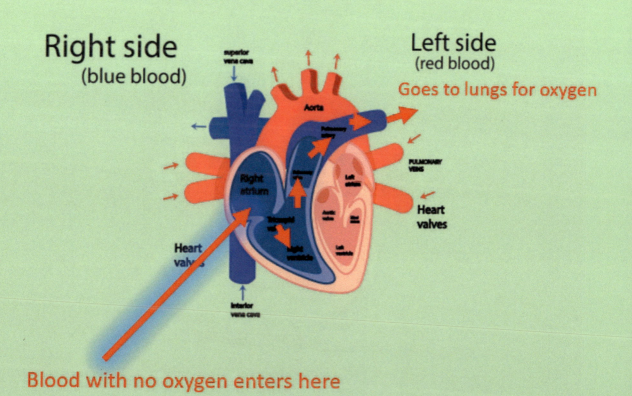

Right side
(blue blood)

Left side
(red blood)

Goes to lungs for oxygen

Heart valves

Heart valves

Blood with no oxygen enters here

What happens when the blood receives oxygen?

Once this blood has picked up the oxygen from the lungs, it will return back to the heart through the left heart chambers into the left atria and the left ventricle.

Heart and Blood Circulation System

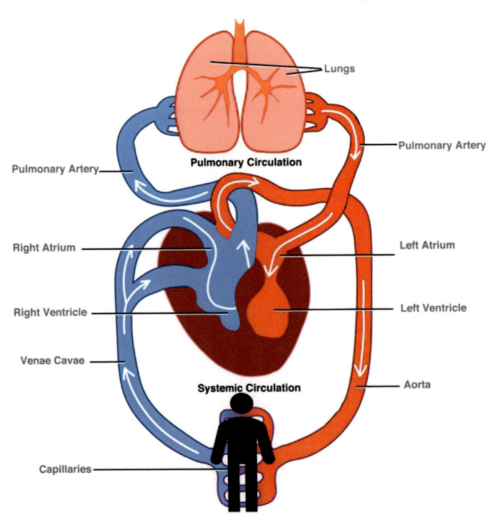

What happens to the blood when it comes into the left heart?

All the blood coming into the heart from the left side is now filled with rich oxygen and is red in color. From the left chambers of the heart the blood is now ready to be pumped out again through the Aortic Artery to carry the rich oxygen into the legs, arms, head, and other parts of the body.

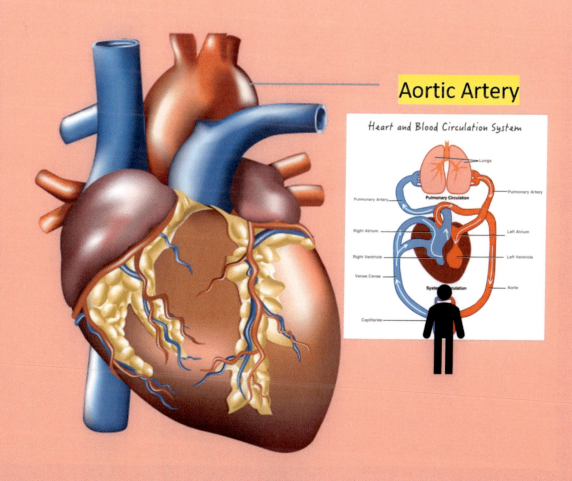

Aortic Artery

14

What is the blood flow process again?

1.   The **right atrium** receives deoxygenated blood from the body and pumps it to the right ventricle.

2.   The **right ventricle** receives the blood from the right atrium and pumps it to the lungs through the pulmonary vein to load it with oxygen.

3.   The **left atria** receives freshly oxygenated blood from the lungs and pumps it to the left ventricle.

4.   The **left ventricle** pumps oxygen rich blood to the body through the Aortic Artery. And the process continues like this all day long.

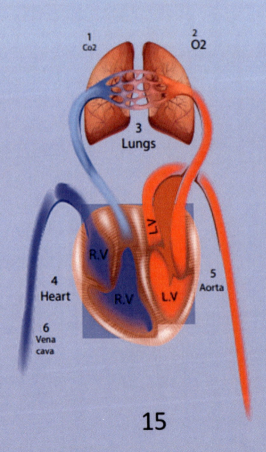

15

What transport the blood throughout the body?

Blood travels through the body through a system of roads and highways called veins and arteries that make up the circulatory system. The circulatory system stretches out across the entirety of the human body.

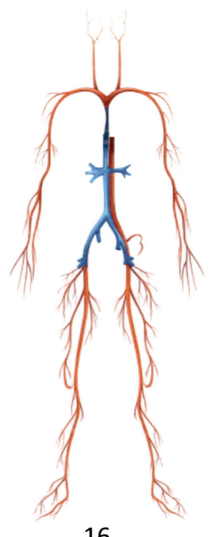

What are Arteries?

Arteries are part of the circulatory system that are red in color because they carry the oxygen rich blood from the heart throughout the body until all the oxygen has been used or depleted. Once the oxygen is depleted the blood is sent into the veins to return to the heart for more oxygen.

Red
Arteries

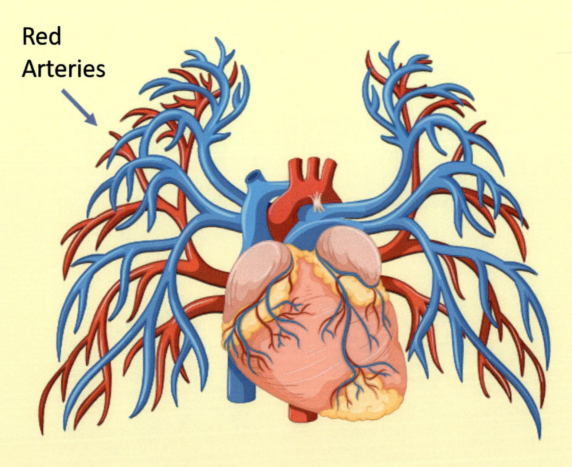

What are Veins?

Veins are also part of the circulatory system but are blue in color for they carry blood that does not have oxygen anymore, but instead carries a waste product called, carbon dioxide from the body back to the heart to be cleaned and removed from out of the body by the lungs.

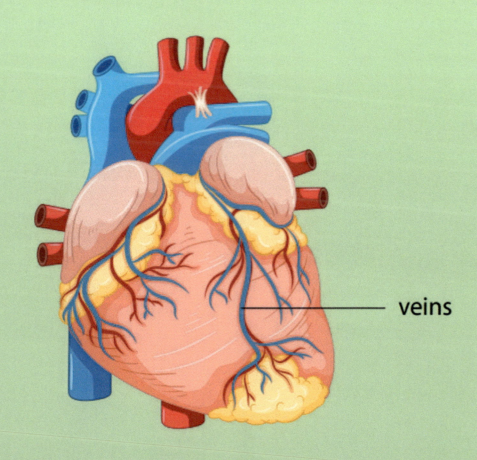

veins

What are Heart Valves?

Heart valves act as small doors at each chamber to control the flow of blood. They open and close to allow blood to flow in and out of the heart chambers. They must close properly to prevent blood from moving backwards through the valves

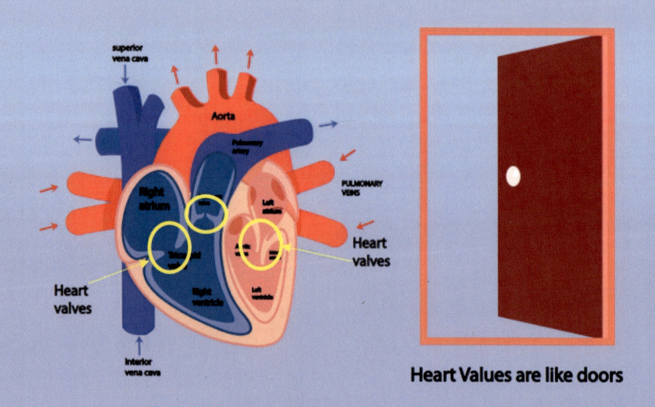

Heart Valves are like doors

What is a Clogged Artery?

A clogged artery is an artery that has something inside it which prevents the blood from moving freely through the artery. Sometimes the clog is created from the things that we eat, like cholesterol. If blood is not allowed to travel through the circulatory system, it can be very dangerous to the human body and can lead to a **heart attack**. A heart attack occurs when blood is not able to move into the heart from the circulatory system.

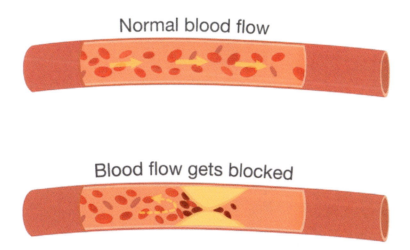

Normal blood flow

Blood flow gets blocked

What is a Cardiologist?

A cardiologist is a doctor who treats and helps people who suffer from heart pains and problems. They provide medications and different treatments for cardiovascular issues. Maybe you would like to become a cardiologist one day.

Draw a picture of the heart and label the parts.

Draw the blood flow direction through the heart (section view picture of a heart)

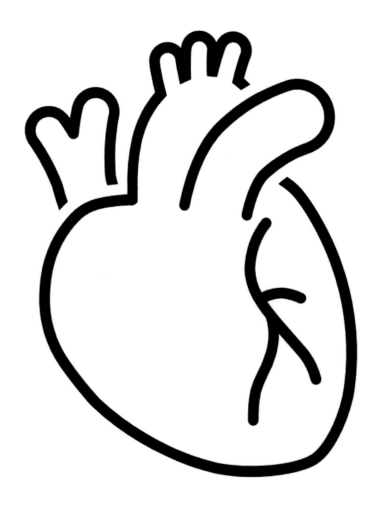

Quiz

Answer these questions.
Write down your answer.

1. How big is the heart?

_____

_____

2. Where is the heart located?

_____

_____

3. What is the name of the bone that covers the heart?

_____

_____

Explain what a heartbeat is.
Write your answer down below.

_____

_____

_____

_____

_____

Select the right answers:

What is a heart valve similar to?
a. A spoon.
b. A battery.
c. A door.

What are heart chambers similar to?
a. Ice Cream
b. Rooms in a house.
c. Bicycles.

How many heart chambers make up the heart?
a. 5
b. 3
c. 4

Write down the blood flow process below

Explain the difference between an artery and a vein. Write down your response below:

_____

_____

_____

_____

_____

Write down your answers to each question below:

1. Explain what a heart attack is.

_____

_____

2. Explain what a cardiologist is.

_____

_____

References

Talley, Nicholas J.; O'Connor, Simon (2013). Clinical Examination. Churchill Livingstone. pp. 76–82. ISBN 978-0-7295-4198-5.

Starr, Cecie; Evers, Christine; Starr, Lisa (2009). Biology: Today and Tomorrow With Physiology. Cengage Learning. p. 422. ISBN 978-0-495-56157-6.

Bianco, Carl (April 2000). "How Your Heart Works". HowStuffWorks. Archived from the original on 29 July 2016. Retrieved 14 August 2016.

Author Bio

The author is an educator and a passionate lover of children. He received his Bachelor of Arts in Biology from Edgewood College, Madison in Wisconsin and a second B.A. in Healthcare Management from Southern Illinois University Carbondale where he also completed his M.A in Engineering. He has a wealth of valuable experience dealing with children of varying age ranges. The author does not only love children, but he understands that when they have the best form of education, it has a far-reaching effect on the wider society. As a result, he is on a mission to make sure that children learn as much as they can.

Made in the USA
Monee, IL
04 June 2025

18784601R00021